THE CAROUSEL LION

By M. Anderson

Illustrated by Lera Derkach

This story is about a special lion who lived in the San Francisco Zoo.

He was not an ordinary lion.

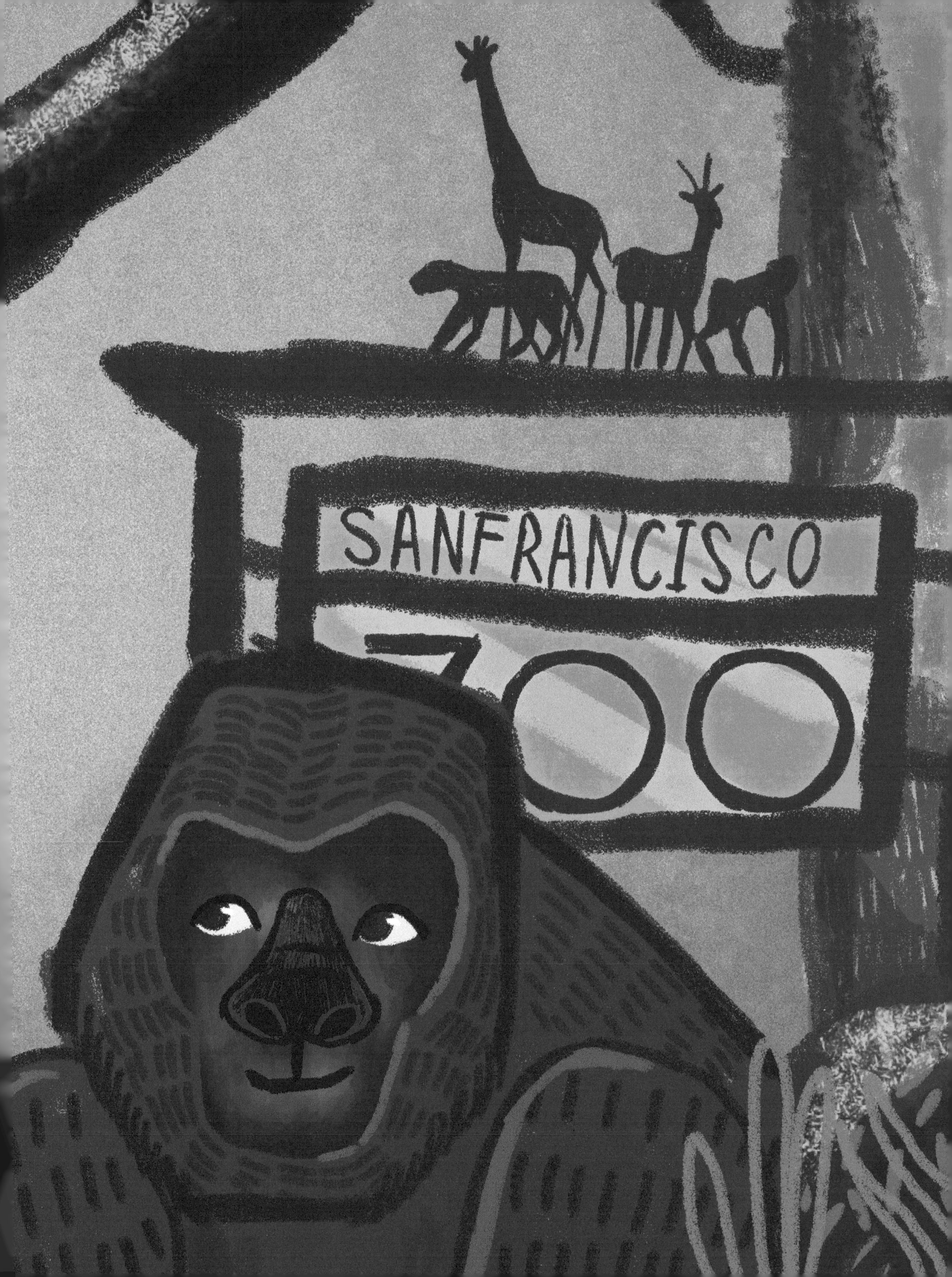
SANFRANCISCO
ZOO

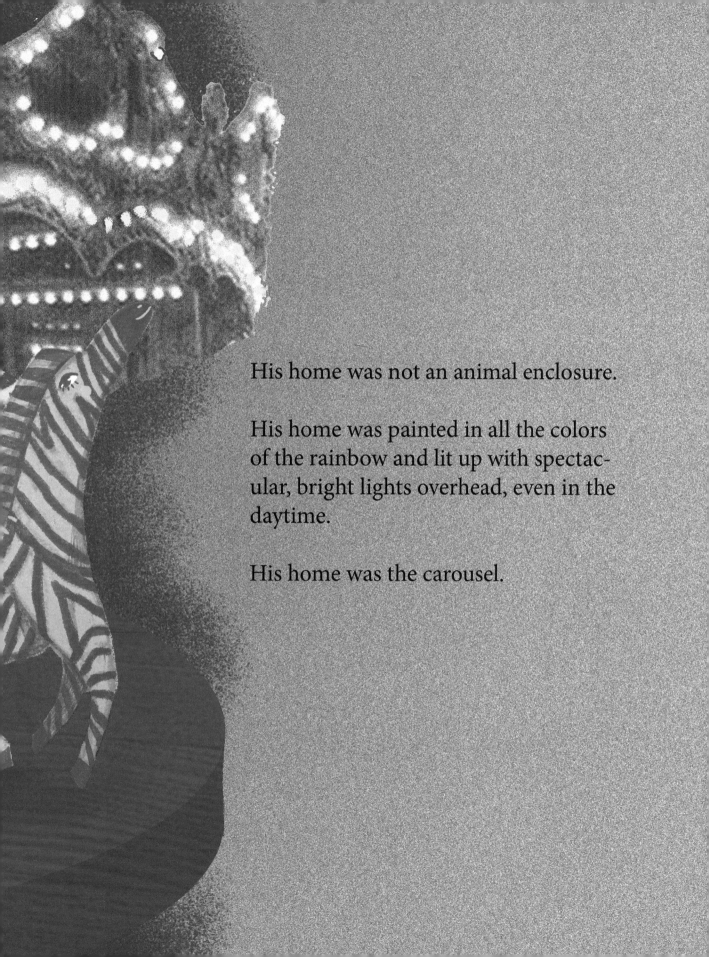

His home was not an animal enclosure.

His home was painted in all the colors of the rainbow and lit up with spectacular, bright lights overhead, even in the daytime.

His home was the carousel.

Lion loved going up and down, and racing round-and-round with his forty nine friends: horses, giraffes, ostriches, tigers, pigs, rabbits, cats and reindeer.

There were even dragons, but Lion didn't know for sure. They happened to be on the other side of the carousel, and no matter how fast Lion went round-and-round, he could never catch them.

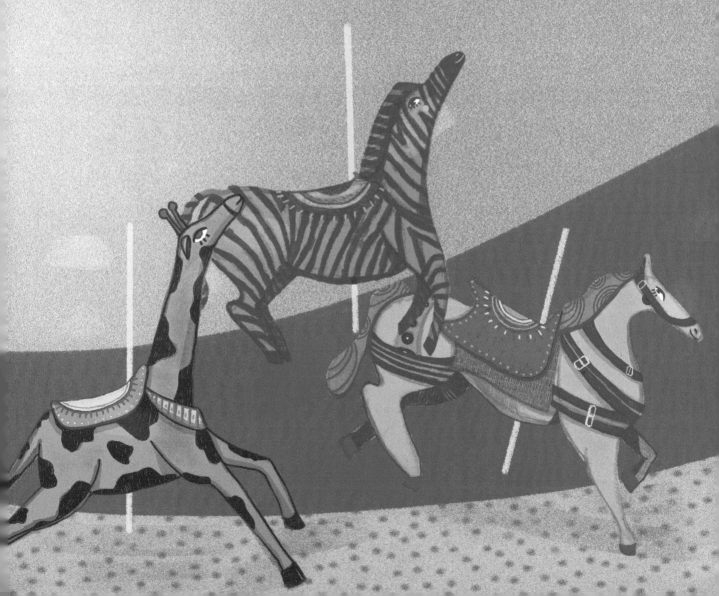

He only saw their tails out of the corner of his eye.

Every morning, Lion really looked forward to the sound of the carousel starting up.

He loved how the dust motes danced in the sun beams streaming in the windows. He loved the cheerful chime of the calliope tunes.

And he loved the feeling of the warm wood floor planks under his paws.

He loved his beautiful carousel very much. But what he loved most of all, was the girl who came to visit him every Saturday morning.

The girl loved Lion too. She was very patient, even when she had to wait a really long time for her turn.

And when she climbed on his back, she always gave him a big hug. She told him all about sand castles, trolleys, fishing, and the Golden Gate Bridge.

Her stories made Lion very happy, and they spent many summers together. With his friend by his side, Lion felt like he was walking on clouds.

But one day, the girl did not come back.

The sun shone, the music played, and the carousel still spun round-and-round as usual.

Lion longed to see the places people went when they weren't riding the carousel, as he wondered what became of his dear friend.

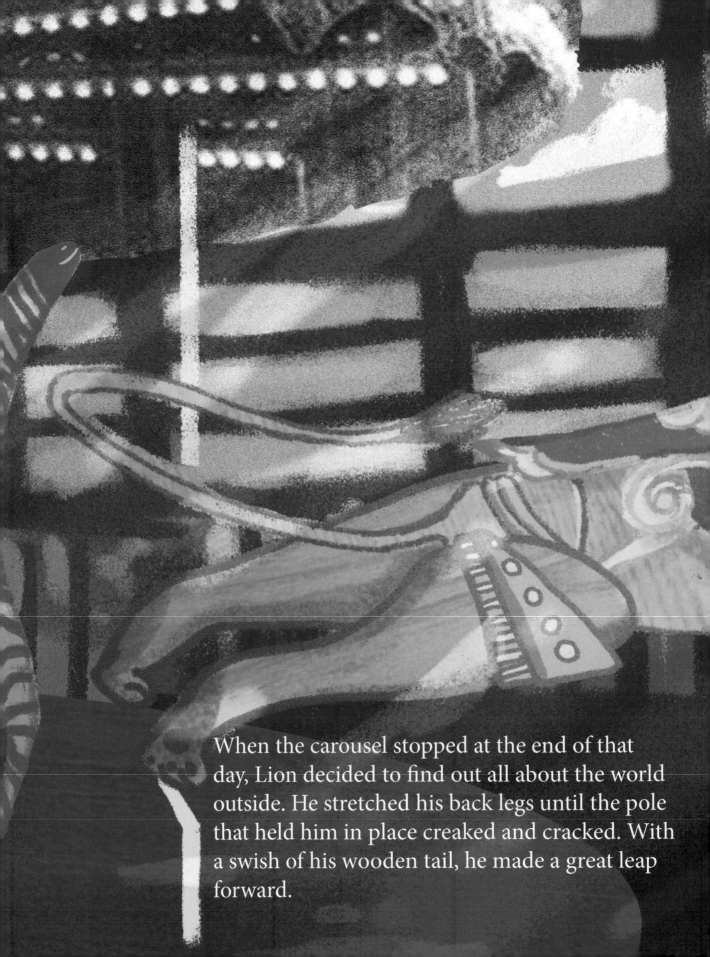

When the carousel stopped at the end of that day, Lion decided to find out all about the world outside. He stretched his back legs until the pole that held him in place creaked and cracked. With a swish of his wooden tail, he made a great leap forward.

How beautiful, thought Lion as he looked up at the sky. Just like the ceiling of his carousel, the ceiling of the world was covered in lights.

He walked and walked until the sky became orange, and he saw a little building with glass sides and a curly-wurly roof.

The little shelter had a bench inside.

Could that bench possibly be for sitting? That was something that Lion had never tried before.

It's fun to dangle my legs, he thought as he tried to make himself comfortable.

But Lion wondered why anyone would sit on something that didn't go up and down, or, at the very least, go round-and-round.

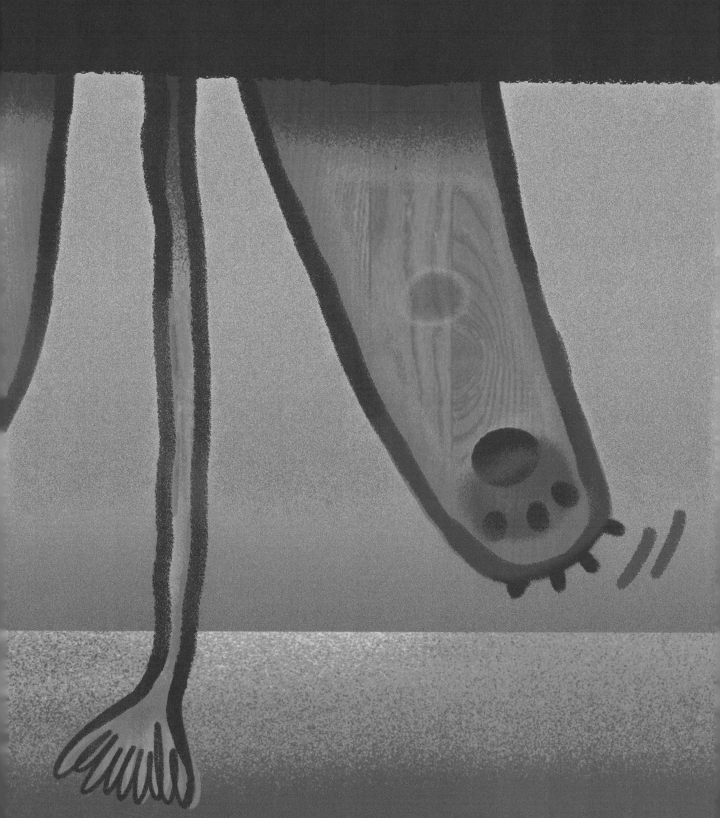

Before Lion could ponder the meaning of benches, he was delighted to see a big red bus pull over right next to him.

It was the perfect time to find out what it was like to be a passenger and practice his new skill. Lion hopped on.

The bus jerked forward, making Lion bump up and down in a familiar way. The road ahead was long and straight, unlike the looping carousel, and this made Lion a little nervous.

Lion held on tight, and squinted
his eyes. Although the faces of
the passing pedestrians looked
nothing like his friend's, there
were so many things to sightsee:

There were the beautiful candy-colored buildings...

Twisty-twirly,
silly-hilly streets...

And of course trolleys, and cars, and busses, and trains of every size...

Lion's eyes widened as the coastal fog parted to reveal the tips of what could only be the Golden Gate Bridge.

He remembered how often his friend visited the bridge and the thought of seeing her again made Lion very happy.

But the girl was not on the bridge,
and the ceiling of the world began to
turn orange.

The bus slowed to a stop in a small
town, where little white sailboats
dotted the bay. Lion smelled the
salty air, and heard the cry of many
seagulls.

The sound reminded him of calliope music,
so he hopped off the bus and followed the
birds along a sandy beach.

First, he walked. And then, he ran until his paws touched water and there was nowhere left to go.

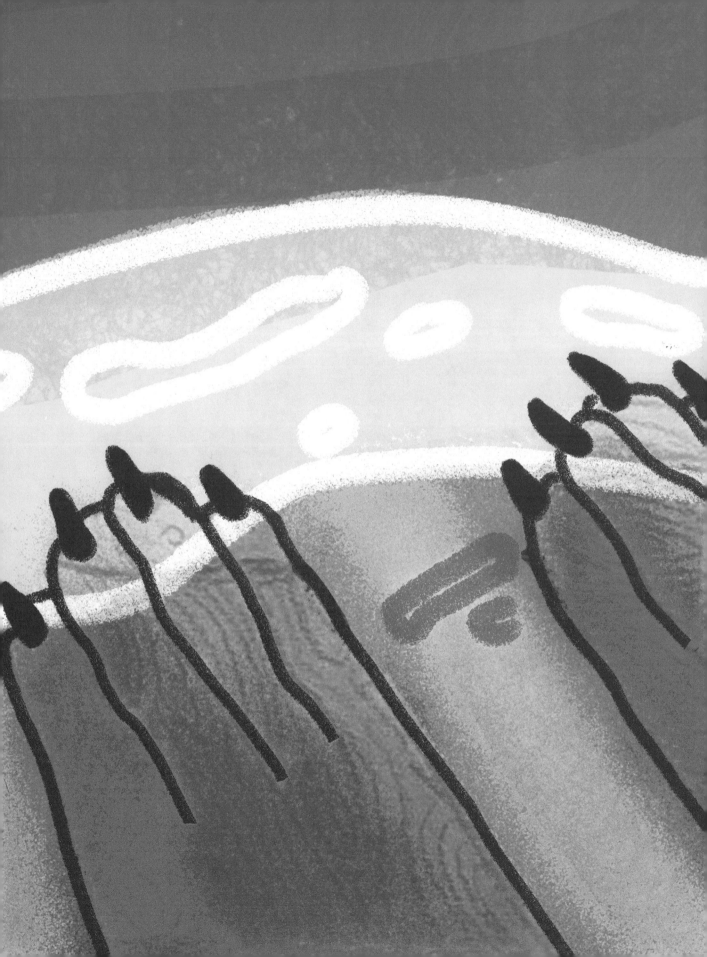

He watched the sun set, and when he finally turned around, he saw that the last lights of the city were winking out one-by-one.

Lion was all alone aside from the fireflies who circled his head.

Lion set his heavy wooden head down in the sand between his great paws, and great tears rolled from his wooden eyes.

His heart felt broken.

He was so tired from his journey that he fell asleep right on the beach and did not wake up when the high tide pulled him into the ocean.

He slept a dreamless sleep, with only the slightest bubbles rising from the holes of his nose.

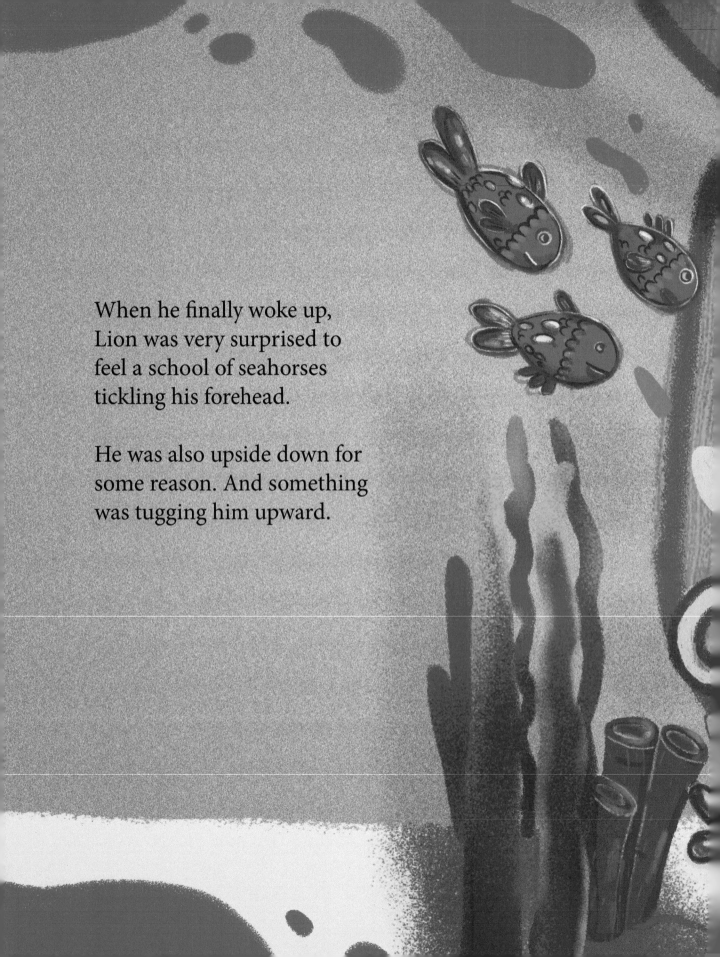

When he finally woke up,
Lion was very surprised to
feel a school of seahorses
tickling his forehead.

He was also upside down for
some reason. And something
was tugging him upward.

After a few very confusing minutes, Lion found himself on a small fishing boat, and looking into the eyes of his old friend.

The girl couldn't believe what she had caught in the ocean.

She touched Lion's forehead with hers and stroked his golden mane.

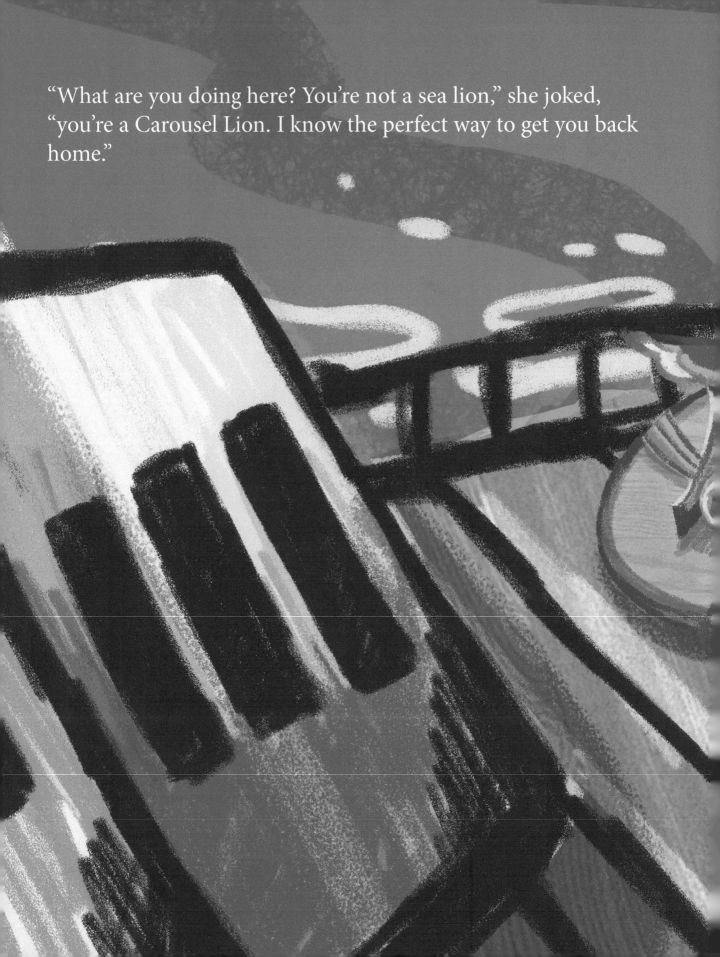

"What are you doing here? You're not a sea lion," she joked, "you're a Carousel Lion. I know the perfect way to get you back home."

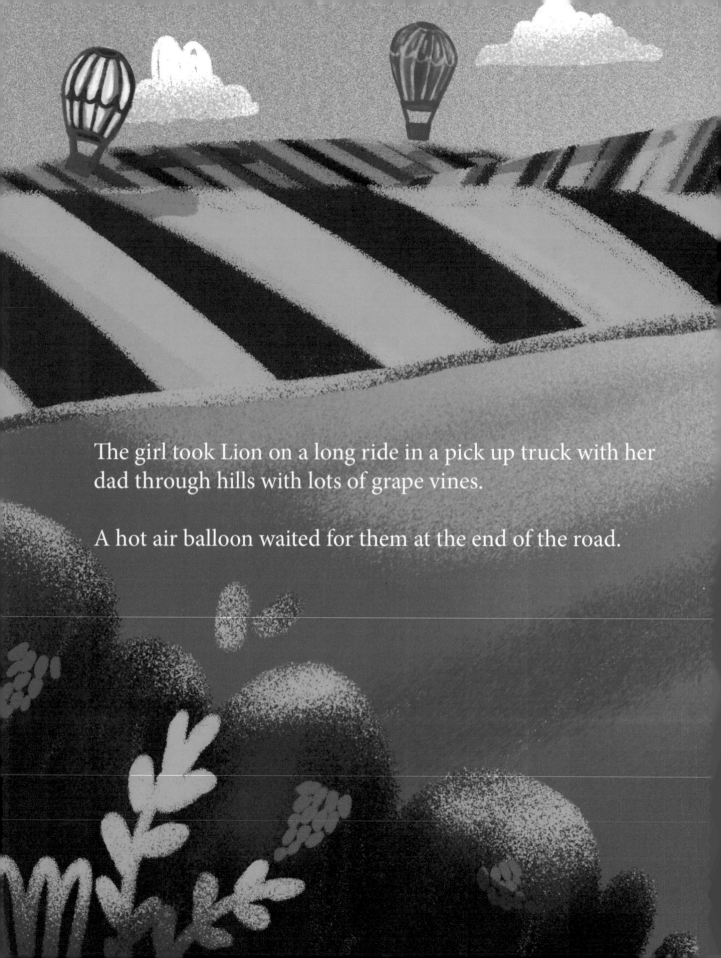

The girl took Lion on a long ride in a pick up truck with her dad through hills with lots of grape vines.

A hot air balloon waited for them at the end of the road.

Lion clambered into the basket and helped his friend drop the sandbags to the ground, as the hot air balloon rose into the sky bit-by-bit.

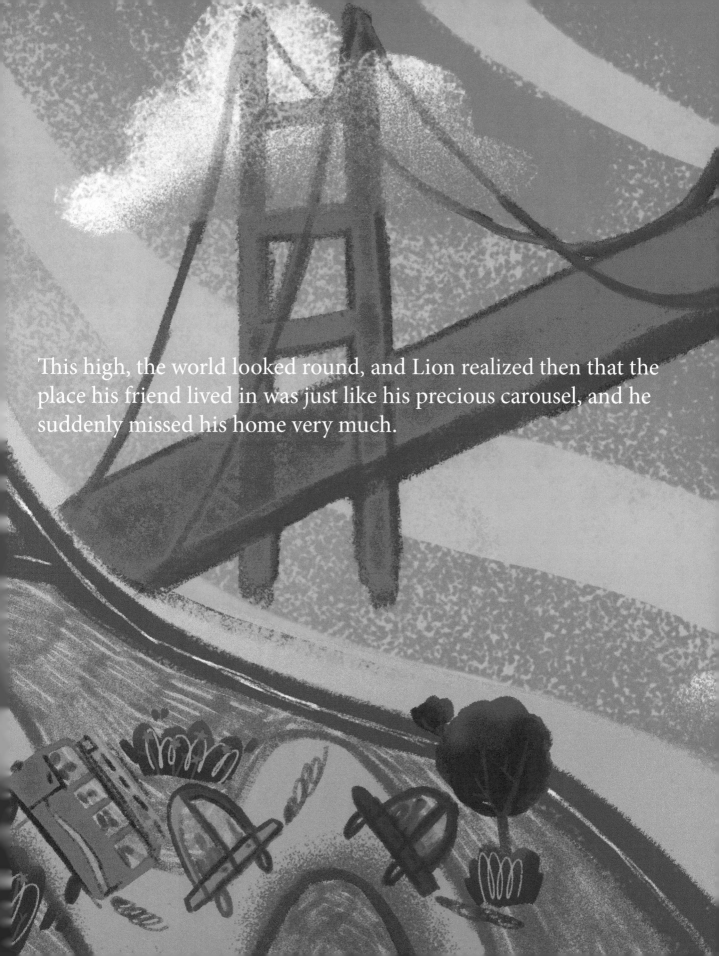

This high, the world looked round, and Lion realized then that the place his friend lived in was just like his precious carousel, and he suddenly missed his home very much.

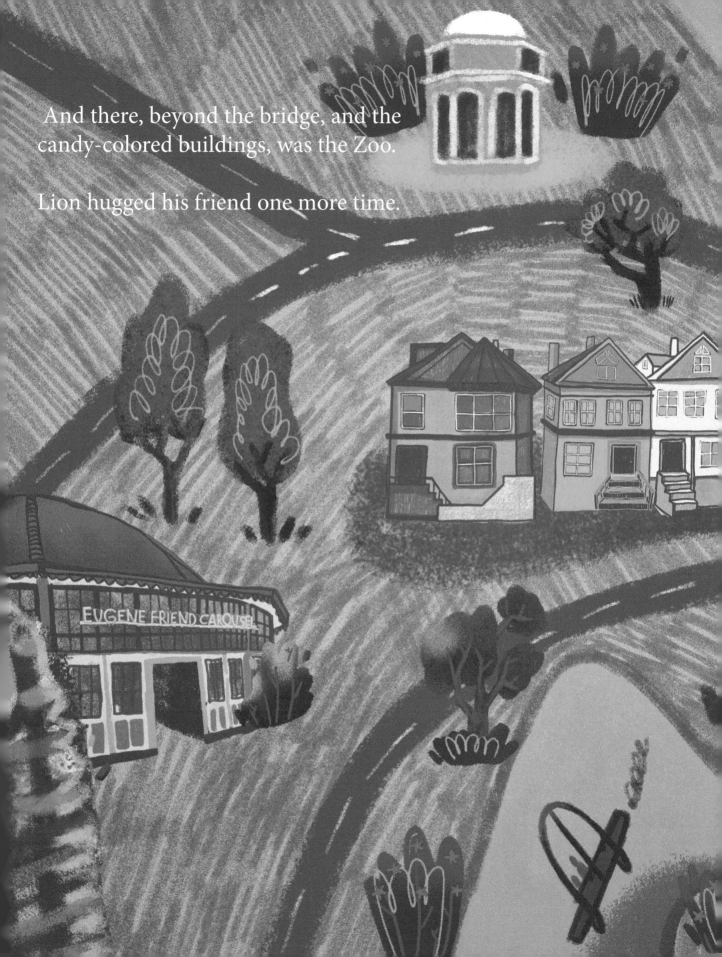

And there, beyond the bridge, and the candy-colored buildings, was the Zoo.

Lion hugged his friend one more time.

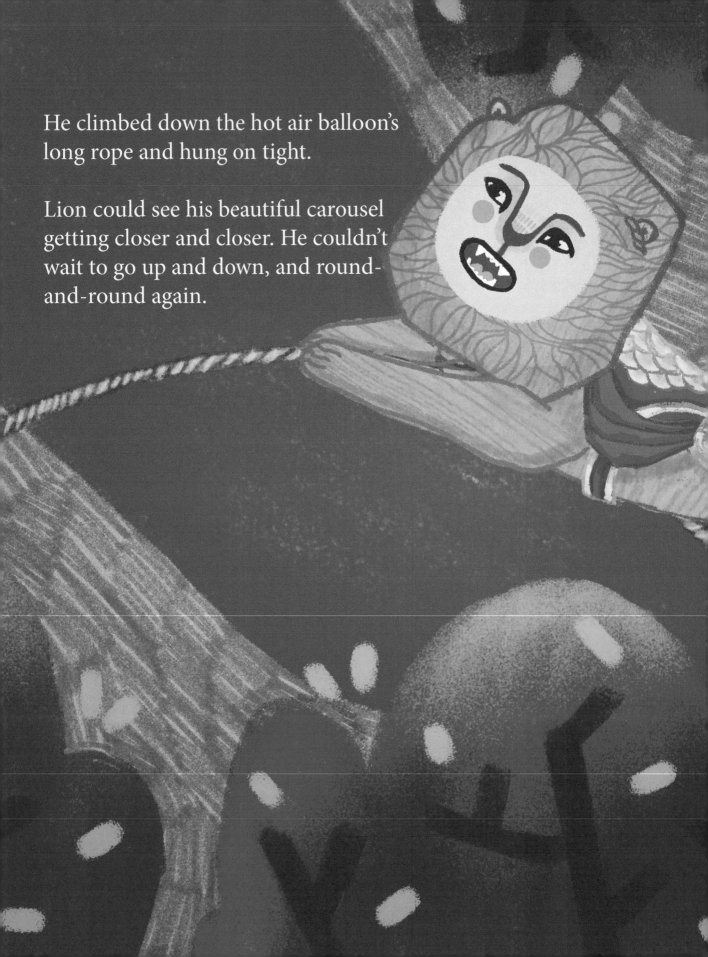

He climbed down the hot air balloon's long rope and hung on tight.

Lion could see his beautiful carousel getting closer and closer. He couldn't wait to go up and down, and round-and-round again.

The End

CPSIA information can be obtained
at www.ICGtesting.com
Printed in the USA
LVHW072204231020
669656LV00003B/12